ANIMAL STATS

SEA LIFE

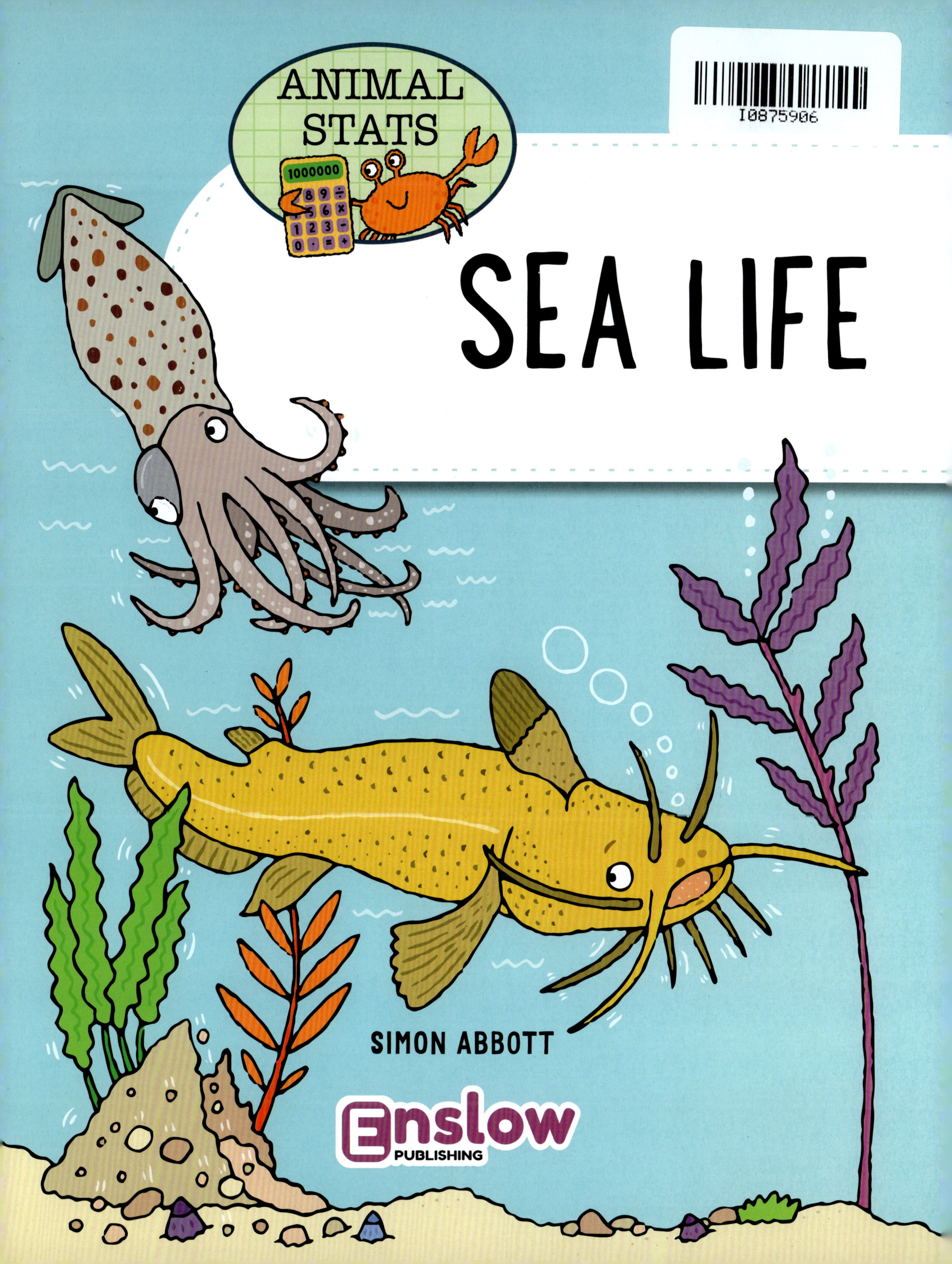

SIMON ABBOTT

Enslow
PUBLISHING

Published in 2027 by Enslow Publishing, LLC
2544 Clinton Street
Buffalo, NY 14224

First published in Great Britain in 2025 by Wayland

Printed in China

CPSIA compliance information: Batch #QS27ENS: For further information contact Enslow Publishing LLC, New York, New York at 1-800-398-2504.

Please visit our website, www.enslowpublishing.com. For a free color catalog of all our high-quality books, call toll free 1-800-398-2504 or fax 1-877-980-4454.

Cataloging-in-Publication Data

Names: Abbott, Simon, 1967-.
Title: Sea life / Simon Abbott.
Description: Buffalo, NY : Enslow Publishing, 2027. |
Series: Animal stats | Includes glossary.
Identifiers: ISBN 9781978549357 (pbk.) | ISBN 9781978549364 (library bound) |
ISBN 9781978549371 (ebook)
Subjects: LCSH: Marine ecology--Juvenile literature. |
Marine animals--Juvenile literature. |
Marine plants--Juvenile literature.
Classification: LCC QH541.5.S3 A34 2027 | DDC 577.7--dc23

Find us on

CONTENTS

LET'S TAKE A DEEP DIVE
AND GET UP CLOSE AND PERSONAL
WITH THE SEA'S SHINING STARS.

We'll meet whales as heavy as **25** elephants,
and marine creatures that can outpace a cheetah!

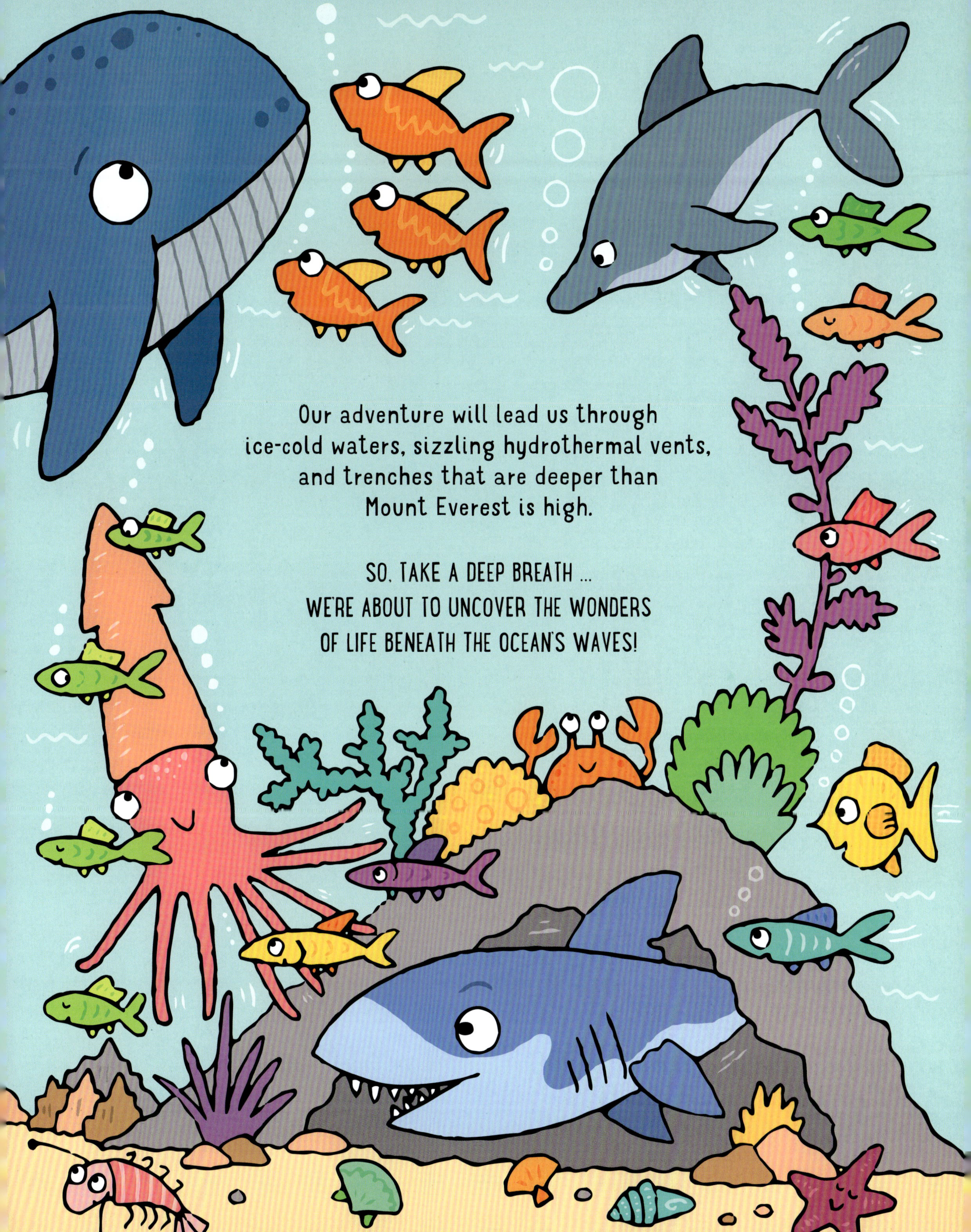

Our adventure will lead us through ice-cold waters, sizzling hydrothermal vents, and trenches that are deeper than Mount Everest is high.

SO, TAKE A DEEP BREATH ... WE'RE ABOUT TO UNCOVER THE WONDERS OF LIFE BENEATH THE OCEAN'S WAVES!

DEEP SEA DATA

Let's get to know some sea statistics!

It may be hard to imagine, but a whopping **71%** of Earth's surface is covered in water, leaving just **29%** for our continents and islands. Out of this water, **96.5%** is found in oceans as salty seawater, while the remaining **3.5%** is fresh water that we could potentially drink. However, much of this fresh water (approximately **68%**) is locked in frozen glaciers and ice caps.

The planet's seawater is shared between **five** oceans:

ATLANTIC OCEAN

The second largest ocean covers around a quarter of Earth

Area:

47 million mi² (77 million km²)

PACIFIC OCEAN

The world's largest ocean covers around a third of Earth

Area: **97 million mi²** (156 million km²)

DEEP SEA DATA!

In total, scientists estimate that there is enough water on Earth to fill a staggering **4,750,000,000,000** bathtubs!

ARCTIC OCEAN

The smallest and shallowest ocean

Area:

9 million mi² (14 million km²)

INDIAN OCEAN

The third largest ocean

Area:

43 million mi²

(69 million km²)

SOUTHERN OCEAN

The second smallest ocean

Area: **12 million mi²** (20 million km²)

Someone who studies all forms of ocean life is known as a **marine biologist**. They can examine tiny organisms through a microscope and navigate submersibles to explore the depths of the ocean floor looking for new and fascinating creatures.

DEEP DIVING TRAILBLAZERS!

Eugenie Clark made an astounding **72** submersible dives and countless more using her scuba gear. Known as "the shark lady," this remarkable marine biologist even took a ride on a whale shark that was **50 FEET** (15 m) long, and made her last dive at **92** years old!

Jacques Cousteau had a lifelong interest in ocean exploration. In 1943, he helped to invent the **aqua-lung**, which helped marine biologists to dive deeper and more freely underwater. Before this invention, divers had to be attached to an air hose that was held above the surface of the water, or wear a bulky and restrictive helmeted diving suit.

While we have identified nearly **230,000** species that live in the ocean, experts estimate that over **80%** of this vast expanse remains unexplored.

It's amazing to think that **91%** of marine life may be undiscovered!

DID YOU KNOW?

Around **2,000** amazing new sea species are discovered every year. Recent entries into the aquatic archive include the fluffy sponge crab, golden cloak anemone, Satan's mud dragon, and the glow-in-the-dark ninja lanternshark!

LEGENDS OF THE SEA

Life beneath Earth's oceans has been evolving for more than **three billion** years.

If we head back **230 million** years to the beginning of the dinosaur age, there was just one supercontinent called **Pangea**, surrounded by a single global ocean called **Panthalassa**.

Pangea began to break apart around **175 million** years ago, creating brand-new coastlines with more shallow water habitats. It also led to the creation of new marine environments, or **ecosystems**, as channels and small land areas opened and warm and cold ocean waters mixed together.

Some species from the ancient Panthalassa ocean still exist in our seas today.

Jellyfish are incredibly adaptable creatures that can survive in a wide range of temperatures. This is why they have continued to thrive in our oceans for over **500 million** years.

Marine snails with distinctive cone-shaped shells called limpets have been a go-to snack for predators for **450 million** years.

Horseshoe crabs have remained virtually unchanged for **445 million** years. Their numerous eyes, hard armor-like shells, and strong immune system have helped them flourish for so long.

When it comes to ancient sea species, it takes a lot to beat a **sponge**! (Yes - they are living organisms!) Fossil records indicate that they have been present on the ocean floor for nearly **600 million** years.

However, ongoing research has potentially discovered a sponge specimen that is **890 million** years old, which could make it the earliest animal on Earth.

Let's get the low-down on some prehistoric sea creatures that no longer dip and dive through the ocean waves.

STYXOSAURUS

This marine reptile, or plesiosaur, about **40 feet** (12 m) long, had a neck that was half the length of its body, made up of up to **72** vertebrae. Humans only have **7**!

TEMNODONTOSAURUS

To navigate through the dark depths of the ocean, this shark-like creature had eyes with a diameter of **10 inches** (25 cm). That's as big as a dinner plate!

ARCHELON

This species holds the record for being the largest documented sea turtle, measuring up to **15 feet** (4.6 m) from head to tail. That's almost half the length of a bus!

KRONOSAURUS

With four powerful limb-like flippers, this massive carnivore could speed through the sea. At **33 feet** (10 m) long, it would hunt large fish, giant squid, and ammonites.

ENCHODUS

Known as the "sabre-toothed herring," this intimidating creature had **four** fangs jutting from its mouth, each as long as **2.4 inches** (6 cm).

ICHTHYOSAUR

This ginormous marine reptile weighed **88 tons** (80 mt) That's **nine times** heavier than a *Tyrannosaurus rex*!

MEGALODON

This is the largest shark ever recorded. It had razor-sharp, banana-sized teeth and jaws wide enough to gulp down **two** adults standing side by side. Don't worry … they're extinct!

OCEAN GIANTS

Our oceans are filled with supersized sea creatures.
Let's say hello to some weird and wonderful record breakers!

CATEGORY: CRUSTACEAN

NOTES: They live mainly in water.
They have a hard exterior body called an exoskeleton.

EXAMPLES: **50,000** species, such as crabs, lobster, and crayfish.

Japanese spider crabs are the largest crustaceans on Earth, measuring an incredible **12.5 feet** (3.8 m) from the tip of one front claw to the other. Can you imagine a crab the size of two beds laid end to end!

CATEGORY: CEPHALOPOD

NOTES: That's Greek for "head foot."
They are invertebrates (no backbone).

EXAMPLES: **800** species, including squid, octopus, and cuttlefish.

If it comes down to length, the **giant squid** is the clear winner of the "supersized" trophy, with an impressive span of **43 feet** (13 m). To put that in perspective, imagine **eight** bathtubs end to end!

However, when judged by weight, its rival for the title is the **colossal squid**, which weighs **1,090 pounds** (495 kg) (the equivalent of **16** labradoodles although it's hard to get that many dogs to sit still on the scales!).

CATEGORY: INVERTEBRATES

NOTES: Animals without a backbone or bony skeleton.
Over **90%** of species on Earth are invertebrates.

EXAMPLES: Sponges, marine worms, and sea urchins.

The **Caribbean giant barrel sponge** measures over
8 feet (2.5 m) across.
Now that would be fun to use at bath time!

Watch out for the **lion's mane jellyfish**. Not only can it give you a nasty sting, it measures almost **120 feet** (37 m) in length, so you'll have to keep your distance!

At **440 pounds** (200 kg) the **Nomura jellyfish** weighs the same as **18** pumpkins!

Among the many mysterious creatures in the ocean, the **giant tube worm** stands out as one of the most peculiar as it has no eyes, mouth, stomach, or intestines. This creature, **10 feet** (3 m) long, lives several miles below sea level, near hot thermal vents on the ocean floor.

CATEGORY: REPTILES

NOTES: Air-breathing, egg-laying, cold-blooded animals with scales instead of hair or feathers.

EXAMPLES: **10,000** species including sea turtles, sea snakes, and crocodiles.

The **saltwater crocodile** is the largest reptile on Earth, measuring up to an impressive **23 feet** (7 m) in length. These massive creatures can weigh a whopping **2,200 pounds** (1,000 kg), which is equivalent to **two** grand pianos! To maintain their bulk, these impressive predators snack on water buffalos, monkeys, wild boars, and even sharks.

Leatherback turtles are the largest sea turtle species, reaching an incredible **6.5 feet** (2 m) in length. Imagine **eight** of these books laid end to end! These amazing turtles can weigh over **1,980 pounds** (900 kg), or half the weight of an average car!

CATEGORY: SHARKS AND RAYS

NOTES: Sharks are fast-swimming fish with pointed fins and a muscular upturned tail. The oldest species is **300 million** years old, and there are over **500** species. Rays have a flat body and large wing-like fins; there are **600** species.

EXAMPLES: Sharks - hammerhead, cookiecutter, great white.
Rays - Southern stingray, common torpedo.

Can you guess which shark is the biggest? It's the **whale shark**! The largest specimen measured **61.7 feet** (18.8 m) - that's the length of a bowling alley! Its enormous jaws can stretch over **4 feet** (1.2 m) wide, but the diameter of its skinny throat is barely bigger than an olive! This means they mainly feed on small shrimp, plankton, fish eggs, and krill.

Check out the giant **oceanic manta ray**. This record-breaking ray boasts a wingspan of **30 feet** (9.1 m), a length of **15 feet** (4.6 m), and weighs in at **3 tons** (2.7 mt). That's heavier than a rhinoceros!

CATEGORY: OCEAN FISH

NOTES: Vertebrates (have a backbone), cold-blooded, and usually breathe through organs called gills.

EXAMPLES: More than **24,000** species including tuna and marlin.

The world's largest bony fish is the weird and wonderful **ocean sunfish**, or **common mola**. These peculiar creatures can reach a height of **14 feet** (4.3 m), a width of **9.8 feet** (3 m), and weigh a whopping **5,000 pounds** (2,265 kg) - that's heavier than the average car!

IT'S TRUE!

In German, this bizarre fish is called **"Schwimmender Kopf,"** meaning **"swimming head."** A fitting name, wouldn't you say?

CATEGORY: MARINE MAMMALS

NOTES: There are four groups of marine mammals:

Pinnipeds: e.g. seals, walruses

Cetaceans: e.g. whales, dolphins

Sirenians: e.g. dugongs, manatee

Marine Fissipeds: e.g. polar bears, sea otters

They are warm-blooded, breathe air through their lungs, and produce milk to feed their young.

The standout star among the record-breaking marine mammals is undeniably the magnificent **blue whale**. Just take a look at these stunning statistics:

- Blue whales are the largest animals known to have lived on Earth (and, yes, that includes the dinosaurs!). They can weigh **400,000 pounds** (180,000 kg), which is equivalent of **30** *Tyrannosaurus rex*!
- They can grow up to **100 feet** (30 m) long. That's almost **one-and-a-half times** the length of a tennis court!
- A blue whale's tongue is heavier than a rhinoceros, and it can gobble up to **4.4 tons** (4 mt) of krill every day. That's the equivalent of you eating almost **26,500** bananas!

- At **400 pounds** (180 kg), a blue whale's heart is over **600 times** heavier than a human heart.
- They are the loudest animals on the planet, and it's thought that their groans, moans, and pulses can be heard by fellow blue whales up to **1,000 miles** (1,600 km) away!

RACE ACROSS THE OCEAN

Let's take a swim and find out which marine creatures are making a real splash! Get ready for the sea life showdown!

In the category of "fastest fish," the **Indo-pacific sailfish** takes home the gold medal. Clocking in at speeds of **70 miles per hour** (110 km/h), this marine marvel is just as fast as a cheetah on land!

The **ghost crab** should claw its way onto the podium as the fastest-moving crustacean, reaching speeds of up to **13 feet** (4 m) per second. How fast can you run sideways?

SEA LIFE STATISTICS!

It might seem strange to hand out a fastest flyer award in a sea-life book, but we'll make an exception for the **flying fish**. They can reach underwater speeds of **37 miles per hour** (60 km/h), before breaking the surface and gliding for distances as long as **655 ft** (200 m).

Can you guess which creature wins the "deepest diver" award? It's the **Cuvier's beaked whale**!

This sausage-shaped whale can be **23 feet** (7 m) long. It was recorded making an extraordinary **2 hour, 17 minute** dive reaching depths of **9,800 feet** (2,990 m).

Let's look at the deep-dive data table:

ANIMAL	DEEPEST DIVE	
Fur seal	1,023 ft	Or five-times the height of the Leaning Tower of Pisa!
Emperor penguin	1,900 ft	That's the same as one-and-a-half Empire State Buildings!
Leather-back turtle	4,000 ft	That's almost as high as the Great Pyramid in Egypt!
Whale shark	6,000 ft	Can you imagine 18 Statue of Libertys on top of each other?
Sperm whale	7,400 ft	Almost seven times the height of the Eiffel Tower!
Southern elephant seal	7,834 ft	That's the same as 88 Tower of Londons placed on top of each other!
Cuvier's beaked whale	9,820 ft	Imagine three-and-a-half Burj Khalifas in a stack!

We've revealed the fastest swimmers and the deepest divers.
But which slow and steady creatures make the longest journeys?

Humpback whales spend their summer feeding on krill and small fish before traveling to warmer breeding grounds to raise their calves. This **4,970-mile** (8,000 km) journey is one of the longest migrations of any mammal on Earth. The humpback whales travel nonstop and survive on the fat reserves built up during the summer months.

In April 2015, a grey whale named Varvara made headlines with her astonishing **13,987-mile** (22,510 km) swim from Russia to Mexico and back in just six months – beating the previous record holder by a mind-boggling **3,219 miles** (2,000 km)!

But it's not just mammals that make impressive migrations: leatherback turtles hold the record for marine vertebrate migrations. One turtle was tracked on a **12,774-mile** (20,558 km) journey from Indonesia to her feeding grounds near Oregon – a trip that took **647 days**. To put that into perspective, it's like making two round trips between New York and Los Angeles!

FLY-BY FACTS

Mini-transmitters attached to the Arctic tern have revealed that this determined flyer clocks up **44,100 miles** (71,000 km) in its annual zig-zag route between Greenland and Antarctica and back! Now that's what you call a frequent flyer!

DANGERS IN THE DEEP!

Among the thousands of extraordinary, breathtaking, and enchanting sea creatures, there are a few you might want to steer clear of ...

The **blue-ringed octopus** is one of the ocean's most toxic animals. Luckily their colorful markings make these **5-inch** (12 cm)cephalopods easy to spot. You'd be wise to keep your distance – it carries enough venom to wipe out **26** adults (but at least their bite is relatively pain free!).

If cornered, the **red lionfish** might try to defend itself with the poisonous mucus stored in its **18** needlelike dorsal fins. You might be allergic to one of their stings, so it's best to stay away!

The **teacup-sized cone snail** may seem harmless, but it has a harpoon-like tooth to inject its venom. It's actually one of Earth's most poisonous animals, but it's not all bad news! Scientists have discovered that proteins within this venom have pain-relieving properties **10,000** times stronger than morphine.

DID YOU KNOW?

Pufferfish contain a poison that is extremely toxic. Each fish contains enough venom to polish off **30** adults, and there is no known antidote. Despite this, in Japan, pufferfish are considered a delicacy and are often served on menus as "fugu." Chefs must undergo specialized training and obtain a license before serving this dish to ensure all dangerous parts of the pufferfish are removed.

With its **10-foot** (3 m) tentacles, it might be wise to give the **box jellyfish** a wide berth! Their harmful venom contains toxins that attack a human's nervous system, heart, and skin cells. Even more shocking is the myth that urinating on a jellyfish sting can help the pain! In fact, it might make it worse (as well as being an embarrassing situation on a public beach!)

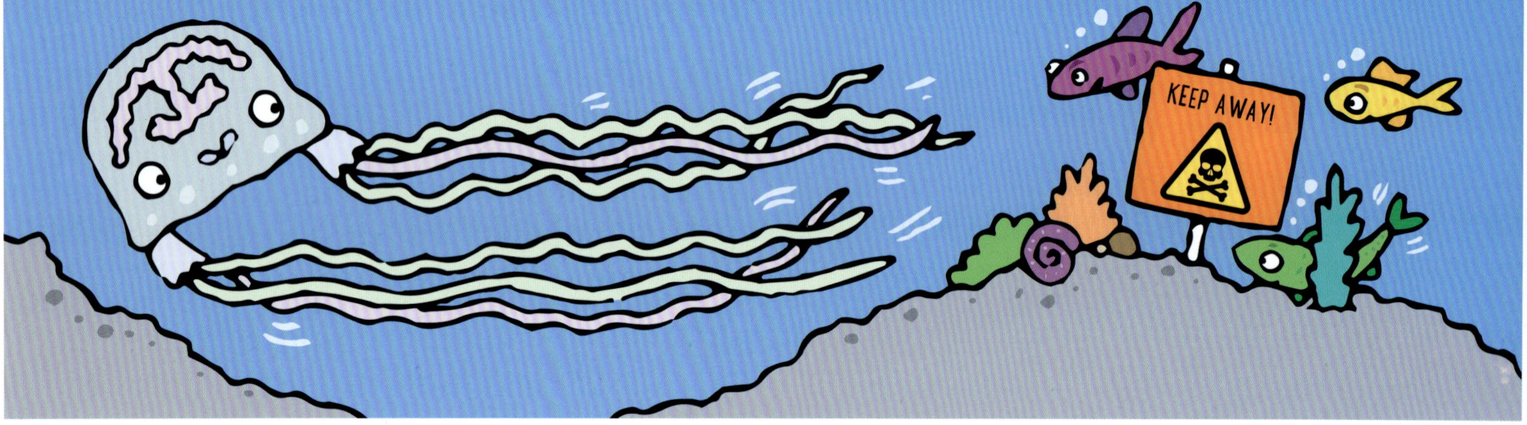

Let's meet the **sea snake**, which can grow up to **9 feet** (2.75 m) long!

The bad news is that its venom is **10 times** stronger than a cobra's. The good news is that the quantity of venom they carry is pretty small, and their fangs are very short. Phew!

Do you want to hear about the most venomous fish in the world?
Let me introduce you to the **reef stonefish**.

This creature has first-class camouflage and is easily disguised among the rocks and coral. It has the capability to inject a venom into its victim through its **13** spines contained in the dorsal fin.
Luckily, an antivenom has been available for over **65 years**. Phew!

I bet you're thinking that an apex predator such as the shark is one of the most deadly and dangerous sea animals.
Think again!
On average, sharks are responsible for only **six** human deaths each year. That's way behind hippos, elephants, crocodiles, assassin bugs – and even freshwater snails.

BENEATH THE WAVES

It's time to explore the ocean depths.
Our ocean is divided into **five** major life zones.

DEEP DATA!

The Mariana Trench is the deepest known point in the ocean. At a depth of **36,037 feet** (10,984 m), you could fit Mount Everest inside and still have **1.2 miles** (2 km) to spare. Our knowledge of life in this trench is limited. In fact, while people have walked on the moon, no one has ever stepped foot at the bottom of the Mariana Trench (although **six** have descended in submersibles).

650 ft

SUNLIGHT OR EPIPELAGIC ZONE

This is where plants such as seagrass and algae can thrive, along with phytoplankton that produce almost half of Earth's oxygen. Encounter sharks, tuna, mackerel, jellyfish, sea turtles, seals, and stingrays in this zone.

650–3,300 ft

TWILIGHT OR MESOPELAGIC ZONE

No plants can grow here due to the dim conditions. See lantern fish, whales, giant squid, crabs, and cusk eels. The pressure here is equivalent to **10** elephants standing on your head.

3,300–13,000 ft

MIDNIGHT OR BATHYPELAGIC ZONE

90% of the ocean is in this zone. No sunlight reaches here – the only light source comes from **bioluminescent** creatures. Creatures that live here often have no eyes, as they're no use in the dark. Fish usually have huge mouths, sharp teeth, and an expandable stomach so they can gobble up whatever food comes along. Specimens include vampire squid, anglerfish, and tripod fish.

13,000–20,000 ft

ABYSSAL ZONE

Animals here must endure freezing temperatures and extreme pressure while surviving on minimal oxygen and food sources. Microorganisms, crustaceans, and mollusks live in this zone.

20,000–36,000 ft

HADALPELAGIC ZONE

This is the deepest ocean zone, found in trenches and canyons, with a constant temperature of **40°F** (4°C). Here, sponges and sea cucumbers feed on decaying plants and animals that sink to the ocean floor.

Let's explore and discover some of the most fascinating marine habitats in the world. Which ecosystems should we know about?

THE GREAT BARRIER REEF

Where? Northeastern coast of Australia.

It's larger than Italy and can be seen from the moon! The Great Barrier reef is home to over **1,500** species of fish. Along with sponges, anemones, snails, lobsters, jellyfish, clams, and **300** types of hard coral, it makes up the largest coral reef system on Earth.

KELP FORESTS

Where? Worldwide, in particular along the eastern Pacific coast from Alaska to California.

Kelp forests are formed by large brown algae that flourish in nutrient-rich waters. Some species can grow up to **1.5 inches** (45 cm) in a single day, reaching heights of **150 feet** (45 m) - almost as tall as the Leaning Tower of Pisa! These forests serve as nurseries for many fish species and provide shelter for sea birds, sea lions, and grey whales against predators and during storms.

DEEP-SEA THERMAL VENTS

Where? Regions of the Pacific, Atlantic, Indian, Southern, and Arctic Oceans, where tectonic plates are moving apart.

Hydrothermal vents are like hot springs on the ocean floor, releasing a liquid that has been superheated within the Earth's crust. Vent structures called black smokers give off a fluid that is hot enough to melt solid metal, emitting dark plumes **180 feet** (55 m) tall. Despite these extreme conditions, scaly-foot gastropods, yeti crabs, vent mussels, and tube worms thrive here.

HOT OFF THE PRESS!

Meet the Pompeii worm – a thermal vent inhabitant. It's one of the most heat-resistant animals on the planet, able to cope with temperatures over **176°F** (80°C). Most animals can't cope if the thermometer goes above **104°F** (40°C)!

POLAR SEAS

Where? Arctic and Southern Oceans.

The Arctic Ocean surrounds the North Pole and is made up of shifting ice sheets. Here, you can find creatures such as **leopard seals**, **colossal squid**, **crocodile icefish**, and **hourglass dolphins**.

The Southern Ocean encircles Antarctica, making it the only ocean to encompass an entire continent. Despite its freezing waters, it is home to **beluga whales**, **narwhals**, **walruses**, and the elusive **Greenland shark**.

OLD TIMER!

Greenland sharks are the longest-living vertebrates that we know of, with an average lifespan of **400** years!
Just think – there could be a specimen swimming around today that was alive during the 1666 Great Fire of London!

These sharks have high levels of a chemical compound in their bodies that acts like antifreeze, preventing ice crystals from forming in their bodies – a welcome adaptation for surviving in cold waters. Brrrrr!

SEA SQUADS

Who are the top contenders for the ocean's "parent-of-the-year" award? Let's take a closer look at what it takes to raise babies beneath the waves.

It might seem logical that the biggest creature in the animal kingdom would have the biggest baby, and in this case, you'd be correct! The **blue whale calf** weighs a whopping **5,000 pounds** (2,268 kg) at birth and measures longer than four beds end to end. Its mother produces **50 gallons** (190 l) of milk every day – enough to fill a bathtub! It's no surprise, therefore, that the blue whale calf gains an astonishing **10 pounds** (4.5 kg) every HOUR.

Male **yellow-headed jawfish** are **mouthbreeders**, which means they hold the fertilized eggs between their jaws for **7-10 days** until they hatch. They constantly juggle the eggs to keep them clean and hydrated, and occasionally pop the whole bundle out for a quick boost of oxygen.

EGG-CITING NEWS!

The female ocean sunfish can lay over **300,000,000** eggs at a time. Baby ocean sunfish weigh less than a teabag when they're newly hatched, but grow into adults heavier than a rhinoceros!

The **female frilled shark** has the longest pregnancy of all vertebrate animals. It can take up to **3.5** years for her to give birth to her pups. Whale sharks can carry over **300** embryos, or babies, at any one time, at different stages of development.

The female **octopus** is one of the most selfless mothers on Earth. She lays up to **100,000** eggs in one go, then cleans them, guards them from predators, and blows oxygen over them. During this process, the octopus never leaves her eggs - not even to eat.

In the case of the **Abyssal octopus**, it can be

53 months

before the eggs hatch, meaning the mom goes without food for over

4 years!

Let's discover the creatures that hunt, feed, and migrate together.
Get ready for a seaside social!

Have you heard of the famous "greatest shoal on Earth"? Each year in May and June, hundreds of millions of sardines embark on a remarkable **930-foot** (1,500 km) journey up the east coast of Africa to reach the nutrient-rich shores of KwaZulu-Natal province.

This jam-packed bunch can span up to **4 miles** (7 km) in length, **1 mile** (1.5 km) in width, and **100 feet** (30 m) in depth, making it the largest mass migration of any species on our planet.

Are you familiar with the **White Shark Café**? This remote area of the Pacific Ocean, halfway between Hawaii and California, is known for its large population of white sharks that migrate there each winter and spring. Once they arrive, male sharks will dive down every ten minutes to depths reaching **1,400 feet** (427 m).

For a long time, scientists were puzzled by this behavior. However, recent studies have revealed that this part of the ocean is bustling with phytoplankton, deep-sea fish, and over **100** species of squid. Truly a shark café!

Next, we'll travel to Christmas Island, located **930 miles** (1,500 km) west of mainland Australia. Every year, during the start of the wet season, tens of millions of **red crabs** emerge from their forest homes and make their way towards the shore to breed. The park rangers at Christmas Island National Park spend months preparing for this event by constructing barriers, underpasses, and bridges to make the mass migration as safe as possible.

When they're not on the move, some sea creatures are on the lookout for a potential mate.

French angelfish form lifelong bonds and often travel and hunt together as a pair.

The male **puffer fish** spends hours creating elaborate circular patterns on the seafloor that can measure up to **190 feet** (55 m) in diameter. The female comes to inspect the design, and if she likes what she sees, she'll lay her eggs in the center of the circle. The male then fertilizes the eggs, then stands guard until they hatch.

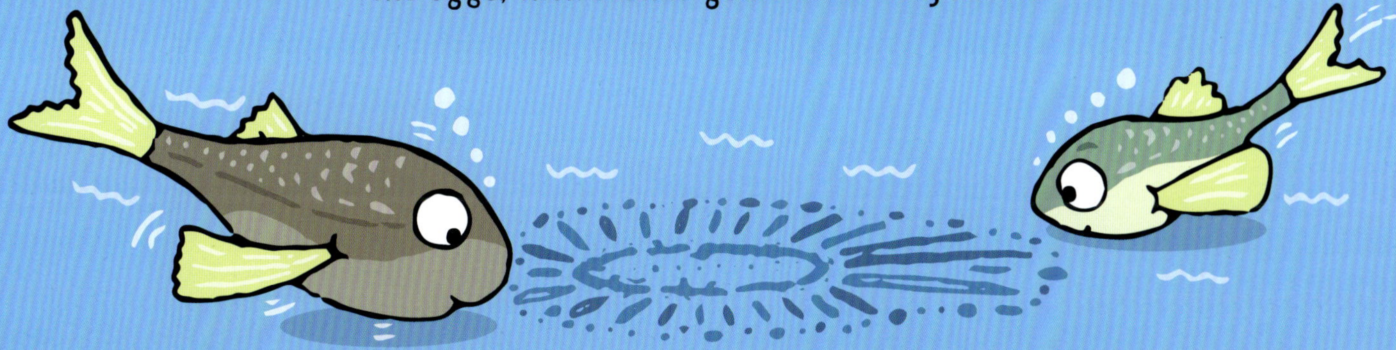

EAT, SLEEP, REPEAT

Let's grab some deep-sea dietary data!
What does feeding time look like under the ocean waves?

It's no surprise that the largest mammal in the animal kingdom has an impressive appetite. Blue whales consume more than **four tons** (3.63 mt) of krill every day, which is even more than a hippo weighs! You probably have some questions, so let's address them:

1. What exactly is krill?

Krill are crustaceans that grow to be about **2 inches** (5 cm) long.

2. How can any creature eat four tons of food?

Blue whales dive down to depths of **1,640 feet** (500 m), then lunge through swarms of krill. Their enormous mouths fill with vast amounts of ocean water, containing countless krill. Then, using their baleen filters, they push out the saltwater while keeping the krill trapped inside. This method of feeding brings in **90 times** more energy than it expends.

3. Impressive! How much krill can a blue whale catch in one mouthful? Around **800 pounds** (360 kg) – that's around **50** watermelons!

WHAT GOES IN MUST COME OUT!

A single bowel movement from a blue whale releases **53 gallons** (200 l) of waste. That's enough to fill your bathtub!

It's time to meet some of the biggest and baddest creatures from the "Hunting Hall of Fame"!

First up, we have the **giant Pacific octopus**, which boasts an arm span of **25 feet** (7.6 m) and can weigh up to **40 pounds** (180 kg) - heavier than a reindeer! This master of disguise can change its skin color and pattern to blend into any background using millions of skin cells called **chromatophores**. And watch out for its super-tough beak made of **keratin** (the same stuff as your fingernails), used to bite and drill into tasty crustaceans.

Next on the list is the **great white shark**. This powerful predator can reach speeds of up to **37 miles per hour** (60 km/h) and has a whopping **300** razor-sharp teeth. The great white shark hides itself underneath potential victims before swimming up and taking a bite.

Leopard seals use their powerful jaws and long teeth to catch smaller seals, fish, squid, and even penguins. They may look cute, and even sing underwater but don't be fooled by these fierce predators. Their technique is to lie still underwater, imitate a rock, then jump out in a surprise attack.

This routine helps to grab them **12** penguins a day!

And finally, we have the top ocean predator - the **orca**, or **killer whale**. With a length of **32 feet** (9.75 m) (longer than a bus!) and weighing in at **22,000 pounds** (9,980 kg), these massive creatures work as a team to corner and catch their prey. Once killer whales have trapped their prey, they use their powerful tails to strike their victim with a karate chop move.

You might be thinking that sea creatures deserve a nap after their energetic hunting trips.

Most fish simply float, or wedge themselves between rocks or coral, then reduce their activity. But **dolphins** must swim to the surface to nap as it's essential that they keep breathing. They also need to be aware of any predators or changes in the sea conditions.

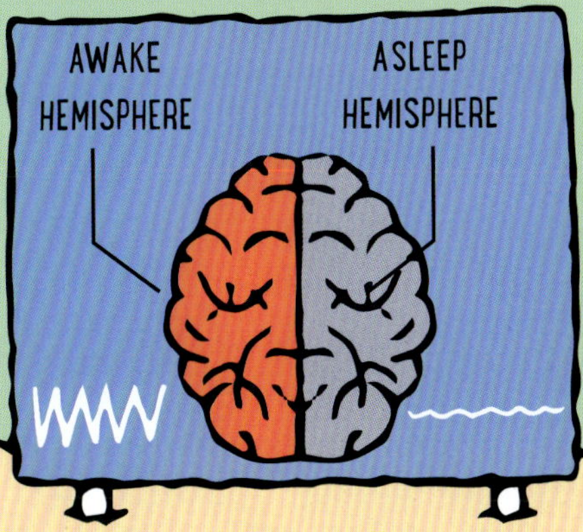

So how do they get the rest they need?

They only shut down **one half** of their brain at a time. When the right side of their brain is asleep, they close their left eye, then swap over after **two hours**. This is called **unihemispheric** sleep.

Sociable **sea otters** hold paws with each other to make sure they don't float away from each other during nap time. Groups of up to **100** otters have been spotted wrapped in seaweed, which acts as a natural anchor to keep the gang together!

The snoozing superstar is the walrus. This **10-foot** (3 m) long creature can nap almost anywhere! Walruses can sleep floating on the surface, lying on the seabed, leaning on a rock, or just hanging from ice floes using their tusks.

On land, walruses can grab a solid **19 hours** of sleep. That being said, there are occasions when they can swim continuously for up to **84 hours**, so they deserve some down time too!

SENSES AT SEA!

Let's see if we can sniff out some sea-going sensing superstars! Shall we feel our way through the ocean depths?

The **yellow bullhead catfish**, also known as the "swimming tongue," has a whopping **175,000** taste buds stretching from head to tail and supersensitive whiskers called barbels. In comparison, an adult human only has around **8,000** taste buds on their tongue.

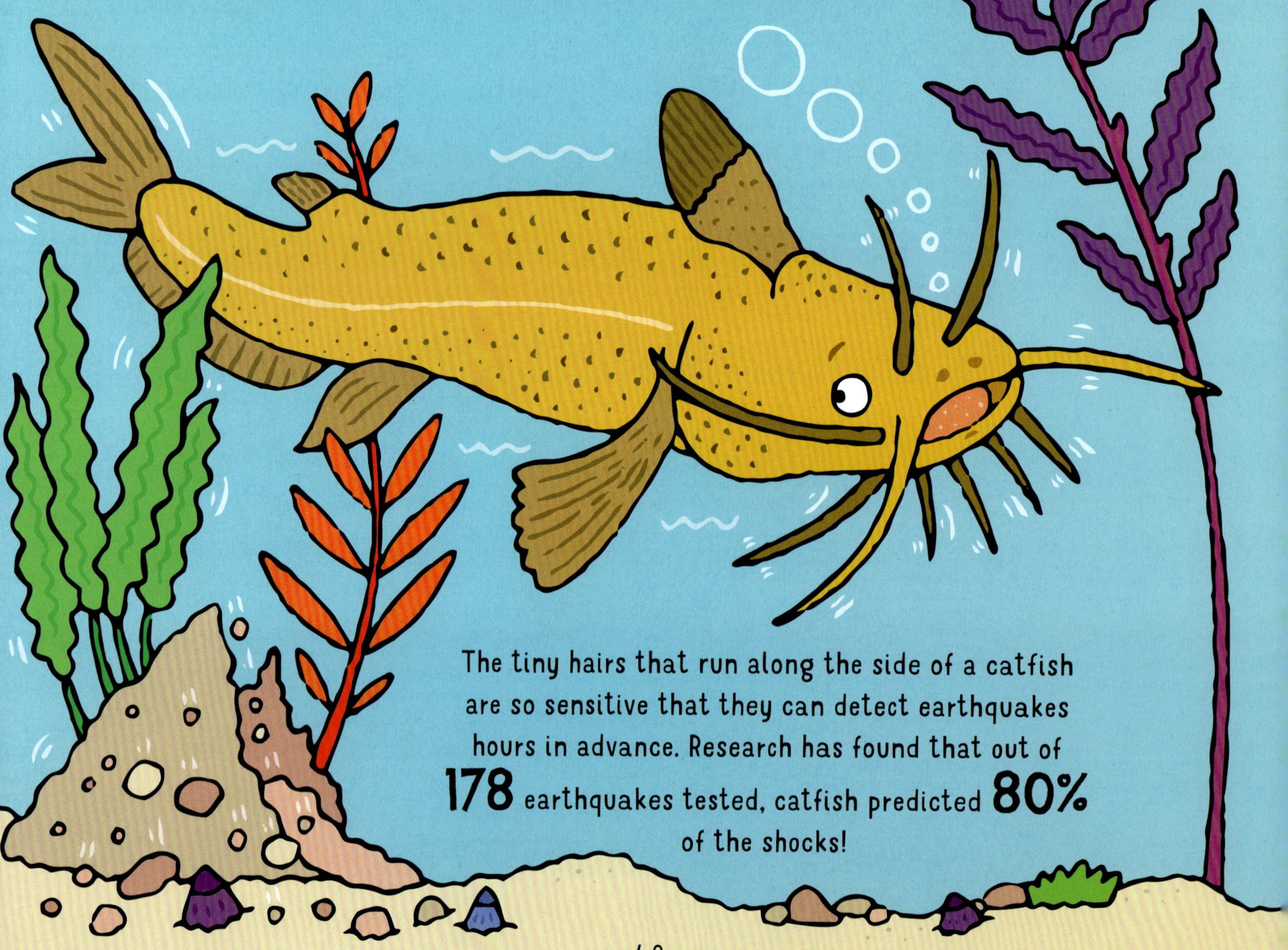

The tiny hairs that run along the side of a catfish are so sensitive that they can detect earthquakes hours in advance. Research has found that out of **178** earthquakes tested, catfish predicted **80%** of the shocks!

Excellent vision is a useful attribute in the murky ocean depths.

The **colossal squid** boasts the largest eyes of any living creature, with a diameter of **10.5 inches** (27 cm) – about the size of a football!

The **four-eyed fish** has, you've guessed it, **four** eyes! This lets this adaptable creature see above AND below the surface at the same time.

The cock-eyed squid has **two** mismatched eyes. One eye is bulging, big and yellow, and can monitor creatures that swim above it. Its other eye is small and clear, and faces downward to detect **bioluminescent** creatures lurking in the dark.

Mantis shrimps are the vision champions of the animal kingdom. Each of their eyes has "**trinocular vision**" – meaning it can work out depth and distance by focusing on three different locations. Most animal's retinas feature **three** or **four** light-detecting cells, or photoreceptors, to decode colors in their environment. The mantis shrimp has **12**!

Whales and **dolphins** use a technique called **echolocation** to hunt prey, avoid obstacles, and find mates. They bounce high-pitched sounds off underwater objects and listen out for the echoes. Dolphins can detect a golf ball-sized object from **325 feet** (100 m) away – that's the length of a football pitch!

The **great white shark** has a better sense of smell than any other fish. Their wide-set nostrils and specialized scent-detecting organs can pick up one part of blood in **100 million** parts of water. This keen sense helps them track down prey from up to **3 miles** (5 km) away. It's no wonder that **two-thirds** of their brain is dedicated to smelling!

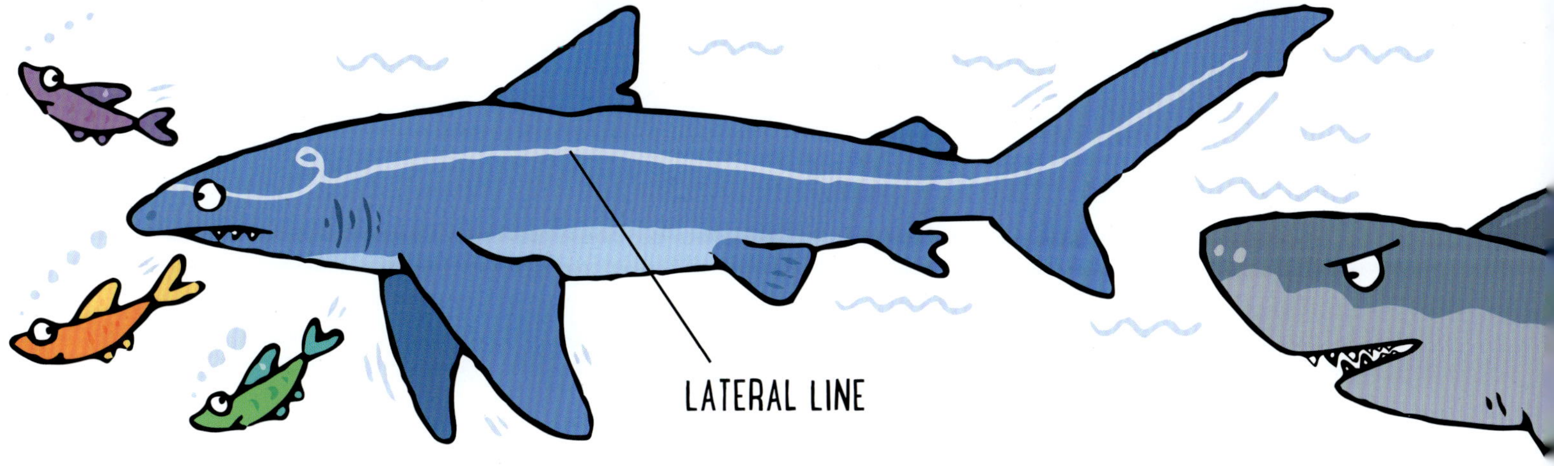

Sharks can also rely on their "**lateral line.**" Rows of small pores run under a shark's skin from its snout to its tail. As water flows over these sensory cells, the shark can detect vibrations in the water.

This super-hunter can work out the direction and speed of its prey from **800 feet** (250 m) away - that's useful when you're hunting in the dark!

WHEN FIVE IS NOT ENOUGH!

Predatory sharks have a secret weapon - a **sixth** sense! They have a network of special cells called **electroreceptors** in their head and snout. These enable a shark to detect the electrical field given off by the nerve and muscle activity of any potential prey - even if they're buried under sand!

Manatees have a highly developed sense of touch, thanks to over **3,000** motion-sensing hairs that cover their entire body. These hairs allow them to detect changes in water temperature, current, and tide strength.

Studies have found that manatees can even sense vibrations in the water as small as **one millionth** of a meter.

THE BLUE PLANET

It is vital that we all take action to save our precious oceans. But what steps can we take to reverse the damage being done?

Our oceans are home to incredible wildlife and amazing ecosystems. They produce **50%** of the oxygen on our planet and provide us with essential resources, such as food, medicine, renewable energy, and minerals.

What are the three main threats to our oceans?

- Oceans are becoming warmer, more acidic, and contain less oxygen
- Sea levels are rising due to climate change
- Overfishing, pollution, and habitat destruction is reducing the variety of sea life, or **marine biodiversity**

Over **2,000** sea creatures are endangered, including **giant manta ray** and **whale sharks.**

More than **75%** of coral reefs in the Atlantic Ocean are under threat, with our acidic oceans bleaching and corroding these precious habitats.

The good news is that attitudes are changing: In 2023, international governments signed the **Global Ocean Treaty,** which will create protected areas covering **30%** of the world's oceans.

Non-profit organizations have been created with the aim of cleaning up **90%** of floating plastic by 2040.

You can help too!

- Conserve water
- Buy sustainable seafood
- Use sunscreen and cleaning products that don't harm marine life
- Clean up your beach litter
- Try to reduce your carbon footprint

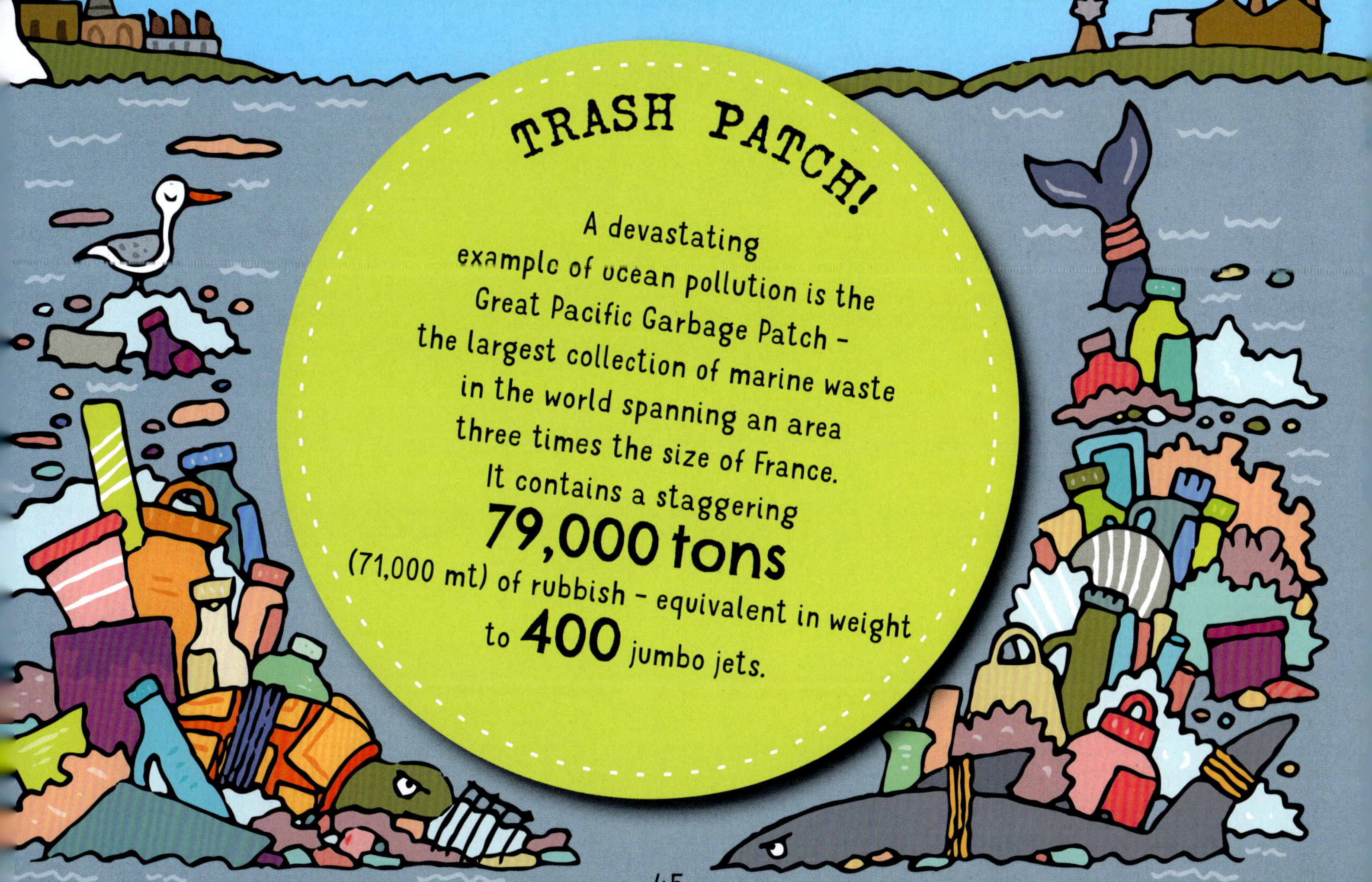

TRASH PATCH!

A devastating example of ocean pollution is the Great Pacific Garbage Patch – the largest collection of marine waste in the world spanning an area three times the size of France. It contains a staggering **79,000 tons** (71,000 mt) of rubbish – equivalent in weight to **400** jumbo jets.

DEEP SEA DICTIONARY

Check out these helpful words from this book, which you could use when writing about your favorite sea creatures!

Apex predator
A predator at the top of a food chain, without natural predators of its own

Baleen
A filter-feeding system inside the mouths of baleen whales

Barbels
Spines or bristles that hang from the jaw of certain fish

Bioluminescent
Light given off by some organisms, including deep-sea fish

Cartilage
A strong, flexible tissue that forms the skeleton of sharks

Cephalopod
A class of sea creatures, including squid, octopus, and cuttlefish

Chromatophores
Cells that produce color and are present in fish, crabs, and cephalopods

Climate change
Long-term changes in global temperature and weather patterns

Crustacean
A class of mainly aquatic creatures, including crab, lobster, and shrimp

Echolocation
The use of soundwaves to work out the location of objects

Gastropod
A class of invertebrates, which include sea snails, conchs, and whelks

Hydrothermal vent
An opening in the sea floor, which releases heated mineral-rich water

Krill
A huge collection of small crustaceans and their larvae, which float in the ocean

Lateral line
A sensory system which lets fish detect movement in the surrounding water

Mariana Trench
The deepest known trench on Earth, situated in the western North Pacific Ocean

Marine biodiversity
The variety of life in our oceans

Marine biologist
A scientist who studies life at sea

Mouthbreeder
A fish that carries its eggs or young in its mouth

Panthalassa
The super-ocean surrounding Earth's single landmass (Pangea) around 200-300 million years ago

Phytoplankton
Microscopic marine algae, most of which floats in the upper part of the ocean

Shoal
A large number of fish swimming together

Unihemispheric sleep
Sleep, when one half (hemisphere) of the brain is asleep and the other half is awake

THE DEEP SEA QUIZ ZONE!

Let's see if you can tell your crustaceans from your cephalopods!
The answers are at the bottom, but no peeping!

1. How much of the Earth's surface is covered in water?
A. 50% B. 71% C. 25%

2. Which is the world's largest ocean?
A. Atlantic B. Indian C. Pacific

3. The prehistoric Megalodon was the largest shark ever recorded. How long was it?
A. 26.2 ft B. 60 ft C. 124.7 ft

4. What is the largest reptile on Earth?
A. Saltwater crocodile
B. Marina iguana
C. Green sea turtle

5. How much krill does a blue whale eat every day?
A. 2.2 tons B. 4.4 tons C. 6.6 tons

6. How fast can a sailfish swim?
A. 37.3 mi/h B. 45 mi/h C. 70 mi/h

7. What is the deepest place in the ocean?
A. Bianchi Burrow
B. Mariana Trench
C. Crillian Crater

8. How much milk does a blue whale produce for its calf each day?
A. 50 gallons
B. 23.8 gallons
C. 14 gallons

9. What are the skin cells that help to camouflage the giant Pacific octopus?
A. Camouphores
B. Chromatophores
C. Colourtomaphores

10. Which creature has 175,000 taste buds covering its body?
A. Blue bottled dogfish
B. Green grilled horsefish
C. Yellow bullhead catfish

11. How big is the diameter of the colossal squid's eye?
A. 10.5 in B. 6.7 in C. 2.8 in

12. How much of Earth's oxygen is produced by our oceans?
A. 50% B. 25% C. 75%

Answers: 1. B, 2. C, 3. B, 4. A, 5. B, 6. C, 7. B, 8. A, 9. B, 10. C, 11. A, 12. A